Hue-Collar

50 Leadership Essentials
for
Humility, Unity, & Equity

By: Gwendolyn Pearce

#writeRIGHT

Kentucky Born and Texas Raised, Gwendolyn Pearce is a Wife, Mother, HR Leader, Poet, Spoken Word Artist, Author, and mayor-appointed Commissioner currently serving on the Louisville Metro Human Relations Commission in Louisville, KY.

She is the creator of #CeeTheWorth, a push to remind everyone to "see the worth" in EVERY person they meet and situation they encounter. To value the person. To value the situation. To work to remove bias and hatred, and to embrace and be inclusive of every person regardless of race, gender, age, personal differences or preferences, etc.! #CeeTheWorth is your way to make the world better each day! The opportunity is in your hands! PLEASE download the song for FREE (from CDBaby).

Book her for your event, order a custom piece, or partner with her to host a workshop or emcee an event for you.

Copyright © 2020 by Gwendolyn M. Pearce

All rights reserved. No part of this book can be used for reproduction for any means, graphic, electronic, mechanical, including photocopying, recording, taping or by any information storage retrieval system without the written permission of the publisher.

Gwendolyn Pearce
Cee'rum V. Publishing
Louisville, KY USA

◊

Dedicated to
everyone who
chose to collaborate
with or work alongside me.

◊

For every person I've led,
thank you
for trusting me to lead.

"I don't want the spotlight, but I do want to be a beacon of light."

— Gwen M. Pearce

Hue-Collar

Plot | 20 Things to Remember When Plotting Your Story 15

1 | "Be the Protagonist" 16
2 | "Set the Stage" 18
3 | "Begin Without Broadcasting" 19
4 | "Take Action" 21
5 | "There's a Gray Area" 22
6 | "Wardrobe Worries Shouldn't Exist" 23
7 | "You Belong in All Spaces" 24
8 | "Don't Just Stand There" 25
9 | "Decipher Between Seeds and Weeds" 26
10 | "Your Pace Wins Your Race" 27
11 | "There's No Catchphrase" 28
12 | "Value the Critics" 29
13 | "Don't Be a Voiceover" 30
14 | "Make Mini Move'ease" 31
15 | "There Are Alternate Endings" 32
16 | "Ink the Deal" 33
17 | "Align the Dream, Align the Team" 35
18 | "A Rose-Colored Lens Fabricates" 36
19 | "Focus on the Vision" 37
20 | "Welcome the Walk-ons" 38

Produce | 20 Things to Remember When You're the Producer 41

1 | "You're Not the Star" 42
2 | "Think High-Definition" 43
3 | "All Data Isn't Good Data" 45

4 | "Embrace the Bloopers" 46

5 | "Don't War Within" 47

6 | "Use the Clips" 49

7 | "Don't Snub People of Their Authenticity" 52

8 | "Make a Hit" 54

9 | "Press Play" 57

10 | "Spark the Spin-Offs" 59

11 | "Go Beyond the Casting Call" 60

12 | "Value the Comic" 62

13 | "Remember the Archives" 63

14 | "Edge of the Seat Matters" 64

15 | "Give the Money Shot" 65

16 | "Special Effects Can Be Unseen" 66

17 | "Make Empathy Part of the Theme" 67

18 | "Don't Be the Bootleg Version" 68

19 | "Passion Not Perfection" 70

20 | "Remember Resiliency" 71

Performance | 10 Ways to Support Ongoing Performance 74

1 | "Change the Backdrop" 75

2 | "Say "Yes" to the Cameo" 76

3 | "Don't be a Spoiler" 77

4 | "Be Honest with Yourself" 78

5 | "Show Time is Now" 80

6 | "Open Up for the Plot Twist" 82

7 | "Interact" 84

8 | "Don't Ad-Lib the Back Story" 86

9 | "That's a Wrap" 87
10 | "Make Real Time Slow Motion" 88
"2020" 91

I've been writing for nearly thirty years. I've been a leader for about fifteen. It seems natural for me to combine the two.

I've been on hundreds of stages, but questioned whether I belonged under those lights; wondered if I was just an extra. Questioning who we are, what we're doing – or *entertaining* self-doubt is one of the worse things we do. It impacts our journey but also that of those whom we're intended to lead. There are benefits of self-doubt; overcoming it builds character. Becoming that *character* is a sign of our readiness for the sequels.

While some might be quite talented, none of us come into our first leadership role fully equipped and prepared to exceed all expectations. We all learn and grow as we lead. There are some things I wish I would've understood ten years earlier. These are things that would've been beneficial to me and those around me had I known them sooner.

One of the most vital things I've learned over the years is to live in color, and lead in my true hue. We must let the hues of who we are guide us in our actions and choices. We're all different, as is the way in which we carry out tasks and interact.

Some things I will spell out in more detail, while others are left for your interpretation. Since we're all h**ue**nique, there's no one size fits all approach to leading. Imagine, you've just completed your first production, congrats on your success! Now imagine, you will begin your sequel right after reading this book. There's no rules to be followed in exactness, but I believe your interpretation of some basic leadership essentials and ideas coupled with your personal attributes will make your sequel record-breaking.

I sincerely hope what I share will help set the stage for some great and unique leaders to *produce* themselves. Many will already know these things, some will already have perfected them, and some will understand them but realize they've been dropping the ball. In those cases, it's likely due to the daily hustle which causes us to focus our eye on the prize. I wrote all that to sound calming, but in my mind, I'm on the edge of my seat to share these things!

I've been fortunate to work with many great leaders, some who admittedly felt intimidated, yet appeared dauntless in action. I admire that, but I know it isn't the case all the time. There are things we have to learn and perfect along the way.

We've all had hits, but imagine the blockbusters we likely would've made if we had always focused on our focus.

Ready. Set. Focus.

Then refocus as necessary.

Before you begin, use this space to list the **hues** of who you are as a dreamer, doer, and leader.

_____
_____
_____
_____
_____
_____
_____
_____
_____
_____
_____
_____
_____
_____
_____
_____
_____
_____
_____
_____
_____
_____
_____
_____
_____
_____
_____

Plot | 20 Things to Remember When Plotting Your Story

> It takes respect to get respect; you deserve respect – so, respect others.
> No matter your dream or achievement, always display **humility**.

1 | "Be the Protagonist"

They say "every day is a blank page and you are the author of your story." So, be the protagonist and push your story forward. Pushing your story forward also means nudging others or moving them forward in the process. You owe this to yourself and to those around you.

A story can't be written without a dream. So, dream! Your dream doesn't have to match that of anyone else. It doesn't have to be shaped like the dreams of others nor have a similar end result in mind. In a world of copycats, please remember your dream should be all about YOU and YOUR vision. Dreams come true when they're authentic. The dedication to achieving your dream can only come from your heart and soul. You deserve *your* dream. You envision it and revise it, and only you can partake in the sequence of activities necessary to make it come true.

Dream anything!

Your dream can be of becoming who you believe you're meant to be or building anything you choose. You can dream of going anywhere you desire or living in the way that you believe is best.

To reach your dreams, you determine the necessary path forward.

Remember, it's your dream and it doesn't have to compare to that of anyone else. More importantly, your dream doesn't have to match what someone else believes is appropriate for you.

Don't let others box you in.

Rather, dream BIG, dream really BIG! And, push it forward.

> "To dream, is to cultivate the future. To care for the future, is to advocate for others."

2 | "Set the Stage"

Every morning or evening, or whenever you start your day is a chance to mentally prepare yourself for whatever the day will bring.

It might not be easy, but do the following two things daily:

1. Practice positive thinking
2. Live in the moment, meaning
    - don't be angry about the past or
    - anxious about the future

Staying vigilant and doing these two things each day will stimulate a continued source of self-encouragement.

3 | "Begin Without Broadcasting"

There's no motion picture without motion. If there's an urge, a notion, or an inclination to do something, *do it*.

I don't believe things just randomly pop into our minds. Rather, I believe these thoughts and ideas show themselves for a purpose. They present themselves to us for reasons which we might not initially understand. While these ideas or urges might seem insignificant at the time, the outcome of taking action may yield significant results – so, do something!

I've heard several successful and deeply happy people who I've come to admire, say things like "the idea just kept resurfacing." I've heard them say they tried to ignore an inkling to do something but it wouldn't leave them. Eventually, they stepped up to the plate, and what was once a thought manifested into something wonderful.

We don't have to share these impulses or ideas with others, especially, when we're still trying to figure them out. I get it, sometimes we have to take time to question things that keep showing up. Our minds are busy machines but there's also times when we have to accept what is intended for us. In these instances, take time to further explore the ideas. Think through it. Stop labeling the recurring idea as a whim. Hypothesize what the result might be if you were to go out on a limb.

For this part, you need only yourself. Take as long as you need. This is where you discover how you feel about the idea. Work with yourself, without soliciting the opinions of others. Thus, you'll be able to reach a deeper understanding and draw your own conclusion before hearing the sentiments of others.

> "Be ambitious in ways that make sense for you, but don't broadcast all your ambitions."

4 | "Take Action"

Be ready to face head-on, the ups and downs you'll come toe-to-toe with while tackling tasks along the way.

If your goals are so big they scare you, then you're on the right track. Of course, this means challenges will come. If it were easy then it would be a way of life rather than a dream, right? Facing challenges while working toward goals might make you feel as though your battery is running low. It's okay to feel tired, but you must be able to recharge, refocus, and restart.

Identify ways that work for you.

> "Take 2 or 2000?
> No matter what, ACTION!"

5 | "There's a Gray Area"

Early in my career, I was highly committed to being fair and consistent. While this is still as important as it was then, I've come to understand there's always a gray area. The only person I harm by trying to see everything in black and white is me.

Applying a black and white lens doesn't remove the gray, it just blinds me to the colorful world around me, the greenness of a situation, the "out of the blue" unexpected needs, the need to get out of the red, and much more. Just like we can't apply a black and white lens to all things, we can't apply a rose-colored tint to everything and assume all will end well.

There's always a gray area! All employees, partners, or stakeholders present different personalities, ideas, hopes, aspirations, skillsets, backgrounds, and perspectives – all adding color to the gray area. No matter the policy or process, trying to put everything into black and white harms the business. So, be willing to work in the gray area when necessary.

"The gray area is a very colorful place."

6 | "Wardrobe Worries Shouldn't Exist"

Many times we've heard, "dress for the job you want, not for the one you have." While I agree to a certain extent, it's imperative we understand that *looking the part* doesn't guarantee we'll book the gig.

Sure, I might enjoy being rushed to see the newest costume design. And, yes, I might love a hip accessory now and then. However, I know that the best accessories are those we don't display but carry inside us like creativity and resilience.

We face many things and come into contact with many people on a daily basis. Looking nice is cool and it likely makes us feel better, but *being* nice makes us feel our best. Mindset, behavior, and interaction are the things that truly move us forward.

> "Leadership is in the application, not the apparel."

7 | "You Belong in All Spaces"

Unless we're educators or school administrators, we likely won't find the "principal's office" at work. Although, across industries, I've had employees jokingly try to apply this title to HR professionals, still there's no principal's office.

Even though, there's no principal's office, we still have plenty of principals. Know your people, your stakeholders, your team, your partners! Respect those with whom you see and interact with often and those you don't.

Seek to understand who they are and what they value beyond the work.

Know all the hues of who you are as an individual, a contributor, and a leader. Having a keen understanding of self and of those around you will better equip you to see yourself as a valuable partner – everywhere.

> "No matter which office or workspace you enter, know that you are never an *extra*."

8 | "Don't Just Stand There"

If ever you find that you don't know where you stand, it is acceptable to take a seat.

One thing I know is you can't succeed without exceeding your goals, and you can't exceed without proceeding, and you can't proceed without knowing where you stand.

Proceed -> Exceed -> Succeed are ordered steps. We can't take them on solidly, if we don't know where we stand. We have to keep ourselves grounded. So, hold yourself accountable for the things you do, and never do anything unless you are wholeheartedly in it or for it.

Sometimes, we have to take a step back and assess an issue to gain proper insight. A full understanding is required because we can't create a hit if we are only halfway committed.

> "You can't make a hit,
> if you're never willing to sit."

9 | "Decipher Between Seeds and Weeds"

It's nice when people take time to share data. By *data*, I'm referring to feedback or opinions *about* us. Often, we have a tendency to want to rely on data that's been given. Most often, this happens when data is wrapped beautifully. Therefore, seemingly delivered with utmost care, meaning, and sentiment. That makes us believe the intended message is a supportive one such as "I want you to succeed." So we rely. Yes, you should be able to accept feedback from those with whom you collaborate. However, the only time you should rely on the data or feedback is when you've removed the weeds and your instinct is aligned.

You must be able to decipher when to rely on the data or when to shy away from it. When you rely on data, you should follow it with actionable items to improve. This is why it's crucial to be able to decode the intention behind the feedback that you've received. This will allow you to identify trill (true and real) development opportunities.

> "Don't allow others to plant things within you, unless it's seeds – that can be watered."

10 | "Your Pace Wins Your Race"

When trying to achieve your dreams, goals, or aspirations, it's never okay to park. With that said, it is acceptable to idle along from time to time, or power run toward your dreams (of course, if you've at least taken part in some advance preparation). However, it's never acceptable to idle to stay beside or run to keep up with others.

Simply put, your pace wins your race.

> "Run toward your dream, rather than running to keep up with others."

11 | "There's No Catchphrase"

I'll admit some leaders just have a natural charm. Charisma may very well be a wonderful trait for leaders. No matter how many times a common phrase might be used amongst the greats, there's no catchphrase for leadership.

I once worked with someone who used the phrase "that's fantastic" frequently. In fact, she said it so often that it made those around her feel they couldn't really get to know her.

She was a terrific employee and an expert in her field but her frequent use of those two words made people question her authenticity. She was very high energy and adopted that phrase to try to convey her excitement about the work. It had become her catchphrase, so to speak. As a mid-level leader, her catchphrase made direct reports, and other leaders feel uneasy. Simply, they weren't confident in their ability to really gauge where she stood because she used the phrase entirely too much.

Be assertive. Convey your thoughts openly; others will catch on.

12 | "Value the Critics"

Don't take criticism from someone you wouldn't take advice from. However, value the critics. I believe we should always let them speak and be heard. While their opinions shouldn't impact your self-confidence or how you feel about your work, they can give you areas for consideration and provide direction for self-reflection. If the information is processed right, it doesn't cost you anything – so, value the critics.

Not taking heed into the words of every critic will ensure you don't give away your power. Instead increase your power by letting those who you admire, inspire you.

13 | "Don't Be a Voiceover"

Always politely and directly express your truth, it's up to others to accept it. Any real relationship or solid partnership should be able to withstand your honesty.

Part of being a leader is being assertive and willing to express not just your thoughts and ideas, but also your concerns. You should be willing and able to express your feelings, standards, and expectations. Delivering material or instruction but having no real voice, means you are just doing voiceovers.

Four tips for assertiveness:

1. Prepare your thoughts in advance, and follow through
2. Position yourself correctly (i.e. sitting at a good conversation distance, leaning in)
3. Make eye contact, smile (if it feels right), and relax
4. Speak clearly, remain calm but use different tones where appropriate

> "The choice should always be to use your voice."

14 | "Make Mini Move'ease"

We often feel guilt when placing our personal needs or work as a priority. It's necessary to teach ourselves that *guilt* is unwarranted. Daily, do at least one thing toward your goals.

Train yourself to trust that it's acceptable to do the things you need to do. No guilt required. Take care of the priorities you've set, and the goals you've established. If you've set a goal, you must love it and believe in it enough to do at least one thing per day which puts you closer to it. As you train yourself in this manner you'll start to *move with ease.*

To achieve our big dreams, we have to do one thing toward our goals each day.

> "Create mini move'ease, and end with the blockbuster."

15 | "There Are Alternate Endings"

I've always appreciated an organization that offered an Employee Assistance Program to its workforce. I've made it a point to openly be an advocate for the use of the EAP. There are so many stigmas out there about mental health. Thus, making some feel uncomfortable in seeking guidance. Therefore, as leaders, let's remind our workforce, our people that it's okay to partner with a professional when necessary.

No matter the type of assistance or support that might be needed, meeting with or talking to a professional can help us reset and figure things out. The conversation alone can help us to see ourselves or a challenge through a different lens. Thus, allowing us to take things on from an angle different than our normal approach.

Those different strokes lead to alternate story endings.

> "Changing the camera angle changes the perspective."

16 | "Ink the Deal"

While being considerate of those around you is imperative, there's never a time when it's right to *willingly* dim your shine to satisfy someone else. So, instead of dimming your shine – try to bring others along. Be highly considerate.

Years ago, as a new manager, I would personally spend days on workforce planning. Simply to plan coverage for a 24-hour call center operation, I took everyone's personal needs into consideration. We had no scheduling technology, only data. I applied so much time and effort into creating schedules that worked for up to thirty individuals. I admit, by definition, I might have taken on too much responsibility and placed too much emphasis on helping employees achieve work-life balance, but I have no regrets. I tried to create schedules that met the needs of the entire team – every other work schedule for our part timers, class schedule for our college students, every school drop off or pick up, every childcare need, every transportation need such as car sharing or public transit schedules, and more. I mean everything. I was being "highly considerate."

I believed that aiding employees in meeting the needs of their personal lives would allow them to arrive for their shifts without worry or distraction. Thus, allowing them to perform better for the business.

Along with being considerate, there are some specifics to remember as you pursue and ultimately achieve your dreams. Achieving your dreams should not:

- involve stepping on others to get where you want or need to be
- involve actions that break someone else down for personal gain
- promote racism or discrimination of any kind
- create adversity for or cause harm to individuals or a group of individuals
- diminish equality or the efforts of others

(And, yes, I still believe that employee well-being is critical to business success. Employees that have less home life worries have less distractions on their minds at work.)

> "Remember the first time you inked a deal? Empower others to ink their deals too."

17 | "Align the Dream, Align the Team"

Building a dream team doesn't require only super-talented individuals be given a role. Rather, it means everyone's focus is and remains aligned. The best part of achieving a dream is simply doing it with greatness. The most pleasure or highest value comes through achieving goals without falling victim to egocentric needs or envy.

Never make personal gain priority; always make team alignment the priority. That's where the dream team comes from. Believing and weaving together.

> "When the credits roll, everyone had a role."

18 | "A Rose-Colored Lens Fabricates"

Not only do dreams change, but teams do as well. Change is part of any relationship dynamic. A team is several relationships interconnected, so expect shifts. Proactively monitor and recognize these changes. See change as inspiration and motivation to lead your team differently.

Teams are constructed of people with ever-changing needs and perspectives. Imagine the team is riding a 5 seat Tandem bike. If one member's viewpoint changes, and they no longer see value in the direction headed, they might stop peddling. A leader needs to be able to realign. If not, the next team member will experience a distraction, and reduce peddling. This will continue until the team either isn't moving at all, or worse – moving with no guidance. A leader can't ignore an issue in hopes that it will self-correct.

Be willing to adapt. Change the lighting, add tint, do whatever is necessary to reset the stage. However, remember it's never appropriate to apply a rose-colored lens and just move on.

> "Applying a rose-colored lens may change the view, but it doesn't prevent the crash."

19 | "Focus on the Vision"

Don't let hidden agendas infiltrate and try to manipulate team activities.

Action items and timelines exist to ensure forward movement and accountability.

Finally, because end goals will change along the way, your team's path, stressors, and dedication will change too.

Remind them to:
- live in the moment.
- not mimic that of another.
- focus on the vision, this increases ambition – no one can take that away from the team.

20 | "Welcome the Walk-ons"

Welcome the walk-ons no matter their role; always be a true collaborator.

Too often I've seen leaders treat differently those who've been with them for a long period. Some of the best leaders, I've partnered with have unknowingly done this; others have done it intentionally. Treating others different just because they've circled the block together a few times just doesn't make sense. Of course, it might be easier to trust those who we've come to know well, but leadership isn't supposed to be easy. We must be able to trust the newcomers too.

Look, not everyone is going to stay for 20+ years. Not everyone is going to stay even five years, but this doesn't mean they aren't going to add value to the business. In some cases, the value they create might extend well beyond the five years they were on board.

So, remember the walk-ons help teams win and advance organizations or projects forward.

How will you display **humility**?
How might you **plot** different going forward?

Produce | 20 Things to Remember When You're the Producer

> Remember, when leading or collaborating, embedding a relentless, harmonious, and unwavering spirit supports **unity**.

1 | "You're Not the Star"

You're not the star, you're the producer.

As you *bring others along*, be sure that you're prepping them to bring others along.

One way to do this is by understanding leaders don't have to solve every problem. Rather, leaders empower others to do so.

Give employees opportunities to be critical thinkers. Delegate or assign responsibility that allows them to use judgment, make decisions, take action, and experience ownership of outcomes. This is one of the greatest opportunities you can give to anyone that you're lucky enough to lead or mentor.

"Leaders create leaders."

2 | "Think High-Definition"

"If you want to *pick my brain*, schedule an appointment." I've often heard this or read it on social media posts of those I admire. While, I understand self-employed artists and business owners have to first provide for themselves and their families, I also understand that there are appropriate times to share experience and skills.

As an artist and author, trust me, I get it, we have to earn a living. However, I also believe we're rewarded when we add value to the lives of others. It's important to give to the advancement of others. Knowledge and skill is a valuable commodity. Please share your expertise and experience for free whenever possible.

Since the year 2000, I've created countless resumes, aided in many job searches, and prepped others for next level interviews. I've never charged for this and I have no regrets. My payment is knowing that I helped folk progress.

My reward is in seeing them climb to new heights. I'm intrinsically rewarded when I see their increase. Seeing them in high definition is all the payment I need.

I've helped at least 10 authors self-publish. I've designed marketing materials for free. I've helped build small businesses that add value to the lives of those in my community. I feel good about these things because I know that many groups have been impacted. I believe that somehow my work is creating equity for individuals and groups.

Help yourself by doing what you can for others. If they ask to "pick your brain," understand they believe you have valuable knowledge that will be helpful to them.

Someone who asks you for time to "pick your brain" doesn't necessarily have the intention of robbing you of information. In reality, they just admire you enough to seek out suggestions or guidance from you.

Knowledge is power. Use your power to empower others. In any field, you can assist someone in becoming the star they were meant to be; this is where you shine.

> "We're not all celebrities, but our actions *can* make us critically acclaimed."

3 | "All Data Isn't Good Data"

For a number of years, we've lived in a technology driven world. Increasingly, data is at our fingertips 24 hours per day. The latter didn't enlighten you; this is something you already know and experience daily.

Regardless of the source, encourage your team to be diligent in how they accept, process, and use information. Not all data is good data. Some things can distract your team or worse.

Data that's landed with us, whether it's opinion or fact, proven or unproven, monumental or minute, impacts us. It's simple – we receive it, and often believe it. Therefore, it's essential that as leaders we lead our teams to weed out the distractions.

As information is processed it should become easier to identify trends we don't need to follow, trends we do need to follow, and those we need to set.

> "Only certain information should make the final cut."

4 | "Embrace the Bloopers"

It's more than okay to get things wrong. Everything will still work out. As a person and a leader, you weren't created to be perfect; you're *not* perfect. So, please embrace all of your visible and invisible flaws. You need to know, it's okay if you sometimes have to hold it all together through the use of all kinds of invisible gadgets and hope.

If ever you're trying to create the illusion of perfection when leading or collaborating, you are doing a disservice to both yourself and those around you. In wins and losses, during mistakes, misunderstandings, or masterpieces, always be as transparent as possible.

"Bloopers are part of the journey too."

5 | "Don't War Within"

Power struggles are invisible to the eye. They're like splinters. They poke and they burn. They can cut you in half, right down the middle, and more. Just know power struggles hurt – bad.

I remember one field day in elementary school, I participated in tug-of-war, and there was no way I was going to allow my hands to be burned from holding too tightly. That's not my idea of fun. Holding on and hurting for a ribbon that will either be lost or stored in a box someday just isn't fun to me. I do still have the ribbon but that's another topic.

Who really wants to suffer? No one. I won't say suffering doesn't have its benefits. We know adversity makes us stronger. Some of the greatest accomplishments are a result of a painful process – so, yes, suffering may (will) be required of each of us at some point in our lives. However, there are times when we simply mustn't hold on, this applies to both our personal and professional lives.

While letting go of a professional hope or idea might not be easy, it's sometimes a necessity. A leader must be able to help the team acknowledge what it's facing and accept it. A leader knows that unwillingness to accept a truth is equivalent to a war within.

I promise it's war; well, at least tug-of-war.

Why do I say this? Once someone's in a cycle of refusing to see or accept something, the mind is already in the game of manipulation. Self-manipulation, which is the worst kind. Minds have different ways of processing. The entire team could suffer if this back and forth, tug-of-war like process continues. It can be both mentally and physically draining for the entire team.

Trust the process.

> "A leader must know when to march, and when to walk away."

6 | "Use the Clips"

Give meaningful feedback – often.

Package it appropriately and deliver it timely. Don't wait until EOY (End of Year) to give feedback, instead select the clips that will best deliver messages your team members need. Be intentional in your efforts to show genuine coaching and ongoing support. Build a connection with your team and with those whom you collaborate by being able to give and accept feedback.

Please don't hold this against me, but early in my professional career, I made a senseless mistake. Nearly twenty years later, I still recall my manager pressing play, and as she exited, I heard my voice mumbling, "I don't feel like dealing with this shit." She allowed me to sit alone in her office to hear how I sounded saying that on a recorded line when a customer placed me on hold. He was giving me a hard time when I simply needed to retrieve information, both he and his wife were talking over each other on two different phones on the other end of the line, I had been sick all day, the work wasn't always inspiring, etc. No matter the excuse, there was nothing appropriate about my comment, even if I knew the customer had placed me on hold to go gather his documents.

I was pregnant with my first child, hadn't been feeling well, and now felt worse and embarrassed that I said such a thing. And, regretful.

Per QA guidelines, there could've been a reprimand even though it wasn't directed toward the customer. The risk of me mumbling anything while on hold, still could warrant a failed quality score. Clearly, my manager was operating in a gray area, and as a leader.

She gave me timely and appropriate feedback, and directive going forward that it could never happen again. I went on to train hundreds of new hires, and more over my four years with the company.

I made a mistake. She made it a valuable lesson.

It may seem small but it left a lasting impression. I've applied similar techniques time and time again over the years. I've shown genuine care for the success of others. I've shown genuine support in times of mistakes and have always given timely feedback in the most effective manner possible.

Sounds employee centric right? Maybe to an extent but it absolutely supports the business. Remember, as leaders, we're the producers of our stories and of additional leaders. In film production, achieving balance comes by light, movement, and everyone working together within a scene. In the business of leadership, balance is achieved by use of proper judgment, decision making, and inspiring people to be the best versions of themselves.

Giving feedback means also giving chances.

Just like I learned a lesson that left a lasting impact, I value that type of leadership. Just like I know that giving meaningful feedback is necessary, I am always open to feedback and appreciate the time, energy, and thought that goes into it.

Feedback is the "tip."
Chance is the "tool."
Tips and Tools are two necessary resources leaders must be well-equipped to provide.

> "Feedback is nourishment; make sure it's tasteful and well-blended."

7 | "Don't Snub People of Their Authenticity"

When you assume everyone's like you, you decrease the likelihood of a successful work relationship. Whether in a professional or personal setting, expecting others to be like you hinders the chances of successful partnerships.

I had a firsthand account of a highly intelligent director hurting her team because she didn't know how to communicate with those who were different from her. She didn't seek to understand or embrace different communication or work styles. Sadly, those who communicated differently were viewed as being unlike her, and were treated differently by her.

Some would say the worst snubs of all time are those who prevented Will Smith, Glenn Close, Spike Lee, and Alfred Hitchcock from winning Oscars. While those folks are more than deserving, I doubt I would call that the greatest travesty of all time. Their legacy still lives.

In my opinion, the worst snubs come to those *regular* folk trying to achieve dreams. Those who work diligently, and give an insurmountable amount of time, dedication, and effort, yet are expected to yield their true selves for the comfort of others. This is snubbing people of their authenticity and it's the most terrible snub ever – every time it happens.

"Never allow others to exploit your team."

8 | "Make a Hit"

Being a leader doesn't guarantee we get everything right. However, it does mean we don't give up. Thus, we may find ourselves in situations where our peace is on the line. You can be thankful for what you have, but being thankful doesn't mean what's causing worry will cease.

In instances, where you feel undervalued or unappreciated, it's okay to let go. Choose the battles you wish to fight for – that includes the option to choose to fight for yourself or your team. Heck, you can even select a partner-in-crime, a "battle buddy" but please know your battle buddy should be fighting for you, alongside you, and never against you – especially, in a professional setting.

Before you start selecting battles or battle buddies. Let's talk about some of your key rights. You have a right to:

- get upset
- disagree
- show frustration
- need a vacation ☺
- take a break

- have a really intense relationship with chocolate ☺
- stress
- feel
- live
- breathe
- grow
- look forward
- look back and reflect
- fail
- be happy
- dislike (but not hate)

The same as you have abilities and capabilities, you have rights. You have a right to all of the things listed above and so much more. The list is endless. Simply, you have a right to be human.

What's tremendously valuable is how you react when experiencing any of your rights. Sure, you have a right to be upset, angry, or feel fed up. The topic up for debate isn't whether these rights exist, rather it's the reaction one might have. For example, you can be fired up or ticked off, but you must have an appropriate reaction. You have a responsibility to others, but most importantly to yourself to react appropriately.

You have a responsibility to yourself and your team to carry yourself not just the way you feel fit but the way you know is right – even when going through a not so great time. When moving forward, your response or reaction will be what defines you. Your team will be watching and making notes. So, be my guest, go ahead and *feel* all those emotions, but do not react to them. Do not live through emotion, instead let your dreams fill you. If the emotion you're feeling doesn't align with your dreams – let it go.

When the highest frustration exists and you feel you can't possibly take anymore, that's when you'll make the right decision. It's in those very difficult times, that you'll choose the right battles. Some will be won and some will be lost, but as we know, "we grow through what we go through." You're going to blossom. In these times, you will create something greater or break barriers by eliminating a wall once built. You're going to forge new paths and eras because you want others to learn from reactions during your journey.

> "We're not proactive 100% of the time; so, our reactions must be hit-makers."

9 | "Press Play"

Letdown is inevitable. People will let you down. At some point, you will be burdened with or changed by letdown, the result is up to you. If letdown impedes your ability to lead your team, then you've failed your team. You must be able to ignite yourself and continue to lead. If you allow something to rip a passion from within you, then you must find a new way to reignite the fire.

You're not the only person who benefits from your ignition. Your spouse, child(ren), students, family, friends, neighbors, pets, a stranger… Others benefit from the ignition that lies within you. Your team and those with whom you collaborate benefit as well. Don't stop!

So often, unbeknownst to us, there are people around us who see us as their inspiration. I promise they just need you to spark once more. It's just like the "pay-it-forward" movement. You can make the world a better place just by reigniting yourself.

Letdown happens but don't let it *happen to change* the end goal. Teach your team to reignite themselves after letdown. Show them the importance and remind them to love their goals enough to never give up, reignite, and stay passionate about the work.

As shared earlier, be as transparent as possible with your teams, actually talk with and listen to them. Schedules are often so busy with competing priorities that we forget what our team members can learn from us, and that we might also learn from them.

Be a servant leader. Remind your team that adversity is a time for caution, but not a time to stop.

Letdown may very well be an acceptable cause for you to slow down, but it isn't an acceptable cause for you to stop.

Reignite.

Keep going.

Your leadership matters.

> "Always have a soundtrack that gets you back on track – or these days a playlist."

10 | "Spark the Spin-Offs"

Spin-offs are the goal. Prepare others to go out on their own to reach new heights, to move into their own greatness. This is especially important when we are serving our community, building programs, and creating access or entry points into them.

In Sales you might hear "always be closing." In leadership, it's always be developing. A leader is always developing him or herself. A leader is also always developing people and ideas! Basically, if you're leading the way, you're creating many paths forward.

These paths go into multiple directions where spin-offs occur likely impacting generations to come. Imagine, the work you do, the projects you lead, the ideas you generate exponentially growing. For example, your commitment to serving others might result in a program that aids in the advancement of an underserved population, that's great. However, what's more valuable is when spin-offs occur and the community sees more programs come to fruition. Thus, more advancement.

Yes!

11 | "Go Beyond the Casting Call"

In 2018, I was protesting in front of ICE after our country began placing children in cages after separating them from their parents at our borders. The day of, I quickly prepared my sign which read "Diversity doesn't work without inclusion." Being an HR Leader for a number of years, I always believed in recruiting and retaining a diverse workforce. However, on this day, when I wrote that on my poster, it was with respect to our country, to our population, to who we are, and who we could be.

That day the meaning was much greater. The phrase never left me, I have used it many times since. It might be my most used hashtag. I realize we always had "diversity and inclusion" in our organizations but I also know that having a diverse team just doesn't work well by itself.

Inclusion is understanding who others are and embracing them. It's unfair for us to hire a diverse workforce and then expect certain team members to figure out what they need to do to "fit in." Rather, we should create work spaces in which they don't have to fit because they are already embraced. The differences need not just be accepted, but appreciation needs to be embedded as part of the culture. We retain team members and partners by genuinely understanding the people we have in place. Thus, we must actively engage.

The uniqueness of a team, department, and company is what makes them special. We must grasp that when we fail to do this, we leave team members to "act" how they feel is most appropriate. This is our failure when we lead them to be impostors. It's demotivating. So, don't just know your cast, love your characters.

> "Diversity doesn't work without inclusion."

12 | "Value the Comic"

A team is a cast. Just like in the movies, members come together from all backgrounds, ages, ethnicities, and more to share a joint effort of creating something wonderful. Everyone has a role. Everyone should be offered a work environment that makes them feel their roles matter.

We must go well beyond casting a diverse group; we must be inclusive. As shared on the previous page, as leaders we must actively engage as this gives us more insight. Thus, aiding in creating ways to embrace differences, embed value for all perspectives, and encourage every team member.

We should value the ones who aim to lighten the mood. This doesn't mean they don't take the work serious. It means they take the team serious too. They believe success comes where there is balance. For this reason, they might often try to entertain others in an attempt to get everyone on the same page.

Explore the ideas and consider the methods of everyone.

> "Don't cease contributions, increase contributions."

13 | "Remember the Archives"

No response is a *POWERFUL RESPONSE.* Always follow up, follow through, finish what was started. Failure to respond is like forfeiting each play until eventually you lose the game. Don't forfeit your credibility and integrity, that isn't the kind of film you want in the archives.

In college, I had a professor who'd often ask a question and then fumble around as if he were looking for something. He simply did this to give students time to think through what he just asked and compose their response. He was empowering students by giving time rather than awkward stares and silence. It's okay for us to fumble like professors we've come across, as long as we know it's our responsibility to finish what we started.

When others don't respond as we hoped, we must still finish our piece. Rushing isn't necessary, but sharing information as it was originally intended still needs to happen. *No response is a powerful response,* so we can't stop in the middle of the game. There will always be an archive of what we did – or didn't do.

> "Finish timely;
> like Nike did with Kaepernick."

14 | "Edge of the Seat Matters"

We've all heard or read it many times, "it isn't work when you love it."

I doubt that any of us have figured out how to end every day on a cliffhanger. So, it might be hard to promise that at the end of each day, every team member will be on the edge of their seat highly anticipating what happens the next. However, you can still find ways to continuously engage them and motivate them.

Get comfortable doing these things:

- Listening to your gut and showing others it's okay to take risks.
- Asking others for ideas on ways to manage upcoming change.
- Assigning pieces of work that align with individual interests.
- Being thankful when others want to lead.
- Volunteering or giving, in silence.

Your team sees everything you do. Getting comfortable in doing these things will excite others, and spark their enthusiasm for the next workday or project.

"Create mini cliffhangers."

15 | "Give the Money Shot"

Rightfully, everyone has expectations and ideas about what outcomes should look like, what work should be like, and more. Your audience includes stakeholders, colleagues, business partners and team members. Give your audience what they *paid* for. In this piece, I'm referring to your partners or direct report, they deserve the money shot.

In most instances, direct reports made a choice to accept a role and report to you. They felt it was the right next step in their journey, so it's your responsibility to meet their expectations. You are the one who can assign resources such as tools, training, coaching, and leadership that they need for success.

I'd never suggest you have to give the money shot at all costs. However, in a partnership, you were selected when someone chose to work with you. The partnership could have been with someone else. For this reason, we owe our partners our commitment to making the money shot, just like we do our direct reports.

16 | "Special Effects Can Be Unseen"

The work must get done. The project must be successful. The outcome *comes* no matter what. These are all facts. Everything comes to its conclusion.

Knowing that there's no way to avoid that an endpoint comes from all action or inaction, it's important that we remember that simplicity can win.

The win shines in its simplicity. Innovation is great but sometimes just producing the promised result is all that is necessary. This is why it's essential to always be straightforward and promote the big picture.

> "Sometimes the special effects are the things we don't see."

17 | "Make Empathy Part of the Theme"

A theme is the inferred stance taken on the central topic or message of a story. Every story has a theme. In some instances, not all involved parties will understand or agree to the same theme.

If this is ignored or not handled in the best way, the team or outcome will likely suffer.

It's important to know that a leader cannot resolve all misunderstandings. Part of the purpose of this book is to equip us with thought processes that make us better at taking action to empower others.

When different stances come into play, as they will, a leader should be empathetic. This means embracing that everyone's journey is different. Then leaders can understand the impact of what they are experiencing and find the best path forward to reset the team and refocus.

18 | "Don't Be the Bootleg Version"

Unless you want to be a bootleg version of a leader, you need to always think before you act or speak. Sounds simple, right?

I once worked with a leader who was swamped all the time. However, she wanted to be first in the region to complete everything. No matter what the new project was, she tried to make certain her team reached the finish line first. This wasn't about delivering; it was about her need for validation which she saw as some form of safeguard. Thus, ideas were often pushed too fast, planning time was drastically reduced, and more. Due to her workload and constant need to move ahead of her counterparts, she often moved at a pace that made little sense. She was timely, but not in a way that worked. She often had little information, and lacked thorough planning. I can recall an ongoing issue with her skimming emails and not being prepared even though she was always *moving*.

I respected her desire to achieve high level results. I think we all did, but we didn't respect moving in ways that lessened the integrity of HR. Moving too fast so she could win a race that existed only in her mind, then having to retract a newly communicated policy or program was confounding.

I support healthy competition. However, her vying style didn't solely impact HR as a business partner but also her relationships. I witnessed firsthand, when her oral or written responses displayed a lack of preparedness resulting in disconnect amongst her peers.

Further, there was an instance where an employee prepared and delivered a requested document. The director didn't thoroughly review and told the employee that he "cut and copied from a website." Had the leader committed to reviewing the document, she would've known that wasn't the case. She likely thought she was doing the right thing, and I don't believe she had ill intentions. However, one who makes these type of mistakes because they're too busy trying to be ahead of the game, will never be a true leader.

Don't risk relationships, take time to connect, make preparedness a priority, and when you don't trust someone admit it – and, fix it.

> "Getting to the finish line first doesn't guarantee you won't be bootleg; refusing to admit when you don't trust guarantees you will."

19 | "Passion Not Perfection"

We've talked about dreaming big and being authentic leaders in this book. Another item that is central to being a good leader is showing enthusiasm. Leaders should go beyond exploring everyone's ideas, and should display high enthusiasm when talking with others about their dreams, hopes and ideas.

Displaying an eagerness to hear others' ideas and an enthusiasm for them, shows team members that it's more than acceptable to work for their passion, rather than working to achieve perfection. A workplace that is unaccepting of mistakes or flaws, means employees often spend time working toward perfection. A deep profound joy can be found when we work for our passions, rather than working to achieve perfection. Imagine the greater results, the improved products, the increased value from the positive effects of working for our passions. Get results by encouraging employees by assigning work that is related to their passions, and not focusing on perfection. Thus, the workplace will experience the most desirable outcomes.

20 | "Remember Resiliency"

I've been inspired by many resilient employees over the years. Resiliency is an excellent characteristic. As leaders, I think it's fair to expect our team members to be resilient. However, it's unfair when employees are forced to build their resiliency by working too long for a bad manager. That is not the kind of resiliency we want or need in today's workplaces. Eventually, it leads to attrition, poor performance, or resentment. "Employees don't leave jobs, they leave bad bosses" is a quote we've all heard or read time and time again. If we know this to be true, why don't we try to manage better?

Increase your team's resiliency by leading from beside them. Show your team that getting sidelined isn't the end of the game. Teach your team members that getting off track doesn't mean the project has failed. It's important that teams collectively understand they can overcome bumps in the road. Resiliency of this type is so important.

> "A leader inspires resiliency, not resentment."

How will you promote **unity?** How will you **produce** future leaders?

Performance | 10 Ways to Support Ongoing Performance

> Remember, no matter where you go, what you work on, or who you work with, sustainable high-level performance requires **equity**.

1 | "Change the Backdrop"

Leadership is quite fulfilling but there will be times when we need to empty to make room for the new. When things no longer serve us, our team or our community, we must be able to make the proper changes.

There will also be times when we're faced with the challenge of not having ownership to change the circumstance. If you can't change it, change your mindset. You might still be in the same place but a new mindset is equivalent to a new backdrop. Thus, you won't allow negative self-talk to persist or repeat the same actions again and again.

> "What you feed will never starve."

2 | "Say "Yes" to the Cameo"

Leadership matters, there's no doubt about that. Inspiration also matters. It's not just important that leaders are inspiring to those around them, but leaders also need to be open and courageous enough to allow themselves to continue being inspired by others.

Be wishful of meeting someone you would enjoy talking with. Be thankful for the opportunities that present themselves to allow you to get to know others.

Be open to allowing the "cameo" appearance. Further, if you were given one chance to have dinner or hold a two-hour conversation with someone, who would it be? Why?

Identifying what you would ask will help you better understand yourself. The conversations you'd like to have can give you clarity where things are unclear.

> "We might not be able to predict the significance of the cameo, but we should be intentional about saying "yes" to them."

3 | "Don't be a Spoiler"

Maintain confidence. Maintain integrity.

Whether it's something sizeable like a new project, a new diversification plan, a new strategy or direction, or something that is more intimate like a personal conversation or shared ambition, it's critical to always maintain confidentiality. Simply put, when someone shares something of a private nature, keep it that way. If it isn't your news to tell, don't.

> "Spoiler alerts don't work in business."

4 | "Be Honest with Yourself"

All of us with any type of dream or goal want to get ahead. This is natural and absolutely permissible. For this reason, we look for creative ways to expand our work responsibilities, to take on more in the office, or in our communities. There is nothing wrong with expanding our expertise or bringing our ideas to others. However, we need to make sure that we're doing these things for the right reasons.

As an HR Director, I once found myself approached by a leader who was devastated after he received some unpleasant feedback. The organization had recently invested a lofty amount of time and dollars into a 360 Review of all leaders. The company was committed to improving company culture and based on recent survey data knew that the leadership team was a great place to begin. To show dedication to this, we sought to first uncover strengths and weaknesses to create tailored plans for members of the leadership team. Across my desk, sat a leader who championed this process, and who was most vocal in supporting this process. However, it became apparent that while he wished for organizational improvement, he thought his feedback was going to be impeccable.

During our discussion, it became evident that even though he championed this initiative, he supported the right thing for the wrong reason. He expected such high level praise that the CEO would be impressed if he glanced across the findings. When he realized the result of his review wasn't a flawless list highlighting all his best traits, he had a really challenging time accepting it.

Even though he'd been a proponent for getting these 360 Reviews approved and a partner in the process, he was unwilling to accept that he too had areas to address. He didn't want to understand the "real hues" of who he was as a leader. Further, he was unhappy that he didn't end up with a fully raving review that could be used to toot his horn to the CEO. It was an awakening for him. Ironically, it showed another area of opportunity for improvement.

> "Don't do the right things for the wrong reasons."

5 | "Show Time is Now"

This book talks about rights and responsibilities that we have to ourselves and to others. So, it's good to know that a flaw, mishap, or mistake doesn't hinder your growth. For this reason, it's imperative that you know you have the right, a moral obligation to yourself to recreate any "first" you want to achieve. You are ENTITLED to these firsts. I can't tell you that you can go back in time. What I can tell you is that you have an obligation to yourself to create the "firsts" that you deeply desire.

Firsts don't have to be largescale achievements with huge audiences. Firsts can be the little things that only you witness. The need is for you to recognize that you are the audience that matters most in your life. Life is super short. You cannot waste your decades, years, months, weeks, days, hours, minutes or even seconds wondering who is watching, pondering what they might want to see, and seeking fulfillment through their applause. Like the popular phrase circulating on social media says, "Work for a cause, not for applause." Well, in this case – you are the cause! And, you are the audience too.

It's likely that you'll be the most critical audience you'll ever face. Why? Don't be so hard on yourself. You may find that you're being overly critical, placing self-blame, or just having a pity party – it's cool. I get it. I've been there a number of times myself (which I'm unwilling to disclose). One way to overcome this is to view yourself as a beautiful box since we are our own personal storage systems. Don't be afraid to open the box containing only pieces of you. I promise there's something in there that will silence the criticism, show you self-blame is lame, or invite you to a party that is way better than the pity party.

Dig deeper within.

> "It's always show time;
> show up and do what you're meant to do,
> even if you're the sole audience member."

6 | "Open Up for the Plot Twist"

The experience found in processing hurt, pain, or disappointment doesn't feel great, but a good cry is just as good as releasing endorphins during exercise. Now, I'd never suggest anyone cry at work but I can suggest that crying has some benefits. After a good cry, a new energy forms. It's a cleansing. For this reason, you must be capable of and willing to cry.

Tears are essential to your well-being. Crying allows you to release things that no longer serve you. Your soul is always on your side but you have to nourish it and give it the outlet it needs. Again, tears are essential for your well-being. They bring you so much stability and this often goes unnoticed. Releasing them is sometimes referred to as a sign of weakness, but how is that possible when doing so makes you stronger?

Crying is beneficial because:

- your outlook changes
- your perception is different
- you reach a turning point
- it's a way of reaching a fork-in-the-road, a transitional place

Simply put, crying is the point at which the plot twist occurs. Crying results in new strength and a new direction. I cannot tell you the number of times that I've given great advice because of hurt or disappointment that I felt, processed, let out, and learned from.

> "Sometimes, you have to give it a *cry*."

7 | "Interact"

Let me get right to the point on this…

Human interaction is *very* necessary.

Many times I've read, "leadership is a lonely road." I believe that can be true but I also know that you can change the way you travel.

You need people! By people, I mean real, live human beings.

- Not robots
- Not connections
- Not followers

Plain ole people. And, if you ask me they are quite magnificent. Throughout this book, you've read about communicating your ideas, collaborating with, and leading others. All these things are important as you plot, produce, and perform. However, I don't believe achieving your goals and leading projects to success will automatically give fulfilment. Temporarily maybe. However, long-lasting and profound joy comes through self-love and loving other people.

Be committed enough to your own well-being, that you're willing, able, and capable of fostering relationships and actually interacting with humans.

Don't hide behind a device, don't be shallow. Converse deeply with the intent to understand. Play with purpose. Listen with love. Be judgement free. Interact intentionally. We must do this for those who live their lives differently than we do. We must accept that we're not all the same and that we'll never be identical in our ways. This is the best way to create genuine connections.

> "The goal isn't to *claim* to have love for others; the goal is to *exclaim* love for others."

8 | "Don't Ad-Lib the Back Story"

Being able to tell your story is significant. You have to know who you are before you can articulate your story. This isn't something you should ever try to ad-lib. There's a lot of weight on not just knowing who you are, but being your authentic self. Your authentic self is the one that others come to trust.

In work or projects, there won't always be time to plan to the depths which we prefer. At times, we won't have a script, timeline, and design – we just have to do it on the go. In these moments, our authenticity becomes even more valuable. When our team members and business partners know us, they are better able to trust us. Trust is one of the greatest tools in challenging times.

> "Struggle shapes us;
> by challenge, we are sharpened."

9 | "That's a Wrap"

What will be your leadership legacy? If you've been lucky then you've been fortunate enough to live life, love others and prepare to leave a legacy. As leaders we have the same opportunity to do such.

At the end of it all, a *reel* will exist. You may remember some memories, while others will elude you. You'll remember some wins and losses, some challenges, some celebrations. What's really cool is that others will also have memories of your leadership, and your impact on them or the community or organizations you represented.

At some future point in time, you become the story. "Once upon a time there was a leader who" will begin the narrative about you.

> "The footage of your life should help others get their footing – *that's reel.*"

10 | "Make Real Time Slow Motion"

Most days there's no time to move in "slow motion." We might accomplish the things we need to take care of but there's not much down time. Same with our goals, we set them, work toward them, and then hopefully achieve them. However, due to the next idea or need, there is little time in between to celebrate the success.

While you can't slow down or necessarily change the pace, or move in slow motion, you can create time to reflect on successes. Create moments in real time that feel like slow motion, where you can be in aww of what you've created or pat yourself on the back for your accomplishments.

At the end of it all, be grateful. At the end of each day, be thankful. Always keep a good heart as good intentions will lead you. Remember, you can't have the picture without the motion, but you shouldn't have the motion without emotion.

Give yourself time to *think* and *feel*.

How will you create **equity** going forward? How will you sustain **performance**?

"2020"

If there's ever a time when you can't see beyond the challenge, remember 2020.

For many (if not all), 2020 will go down in history as the year of pivot. Not just doctors or medical staff, not just business or HR leaders but teachers, business owners, artists, entrepreneurs, and more all faced something never experienced. We all faced it with determination, hope, compassion, and resilience. Together, we learned that the challenges of 2020 go beyond a shift or pivot, and we will never be the same.

As leaders, we tried. As individuals, we continued to evolve.

Together, we learned more about ourselves. Together, we overcame.

Parents, families, entire communities, and all the systems within them had to change almost instantly. While working as one, we reconnected with each other. While being apart, we found gratitude, and unity.

We fought, we embarked, we embraced. We traveled back in time and hoped for a future. We took on two necessary journeys that required different directions. One that required sacrifice in our homes, one that required sacrifice outside of them. Both equally important and urgent.

We masked to fight madness
...and it wasn't a masquerade.

We caravanned, the year
...gave us no need to parade.

[h**Ue**NITY – Understanding the hues of who we are, and leading with "unity" as the goal.]

For contact or booking information
Email: HueCollarLeader@gmail.com

www.ingramcontent.com/pod-product-compliance
Lightning Source LLC
Chambersburg PA
CBHW051537240526
45465CB00027B/596